Taxes and

S-Corp

What it is and How it can Save You a lot of Money

Paden Squires, CPA

# Table of Contents

# Introduction

For some of us who do not find the regular job satisfying enough, becoming an entrepreneur provides us with the prospect of creating a better position for ourselves and the people who mean so much to us. The ability to establish your own company, become your own boss, chase the dreams you have always had within yourself are all things entrepreneurship can provide.

It's little wonder over 30 million Americans pursue entrepreneurship today, per the U.S. Census Bureau of Labor Statistics. That said, being a successful business owner requires a tremendous amount of sacrifice and dedication to your hustle as well as carefully determining the direction in which to steer your business.

As your business starts to grow, you will be faced with the realities of taxes. To be able to navigate the business environment successfully, you need a business structure that offers significant tax advantages while still allowing you to enjoy the flexibility and benefits of being an entrepreneur. The structure of your business ownership can mean major differences in taxes, number of owners, and asset protection.

An S-Corporation, or S-Corp as it is most often called, is one of the more popular choices for entrepreneurs seeking to incorporate their business. Other options include C Corporations and Limited Liability Companies (LLCs) or just operating as a sole proprietor.

Whether you are dreaming of starting your own business, just starting a business, or thinking of changing your business from an existing structure such as Sole Proprietor or General Partnership, this book simplifies and provides everything you need to know about the S Corp business structure so that you can make an informed decision.

# Chapter One

## What is an S-Corp?

An S Corporation is a business entity that allows income and losses to pass through to its shareholders, and the profit which each of the shareholders receives is then taxed on their (shareholders') personal tax returns at their individual tax rates.

The S Corporation is considered a pass-through entity because all profits and losses of the corporation pass through directly to the shareholders' tax returns. The practice helps ensures that the business' gains are only taxed once – at the shareholder level. Not having to pay corporate income tax on the profits of the company means that S Corps avoid double taxation.

S corps are often seen as the more attractive structure to small-business owners than other forms of business ownership structure like C corporation due to the tax advantages that they offer, all while providing business owners with the benefit of the liability protection of a corporation.

A business entity must meet specific requirements to be eligible for a subchapter S election. These include:

1.	There must be no more than 100 shareholders (shareholders must be US citizens or residents). A husband and wife count as one shareholder in this scenario.

2.	Only individuals, some trusts, some partnerships, estates, and tax-exempt charitable organizations may be shareholders. Other S corporations can also be shareholders, provided only the other S corporation is the sole shareholder. This means that to be an S Corp, you can't have entities like partnerships or corporations as investors.

Being an S Corporation also provides your business with greater flexibility such as the ability to use the cash method of accounting rather than the accrual method if you do not have inventory. The cash method is simple, reliable, and fast. Under the cash method of accounting, income is taxable when received, and expenses are deductible when paid.

Other than these, S corporations adhere to the same guidelines as other corporations, and this often results in higher legal and tax service costs. S-Corps are also required to file articles of incorporation, hold directors and shareholders meetings, keep corporate minutes, as well as allow shareholders to vote on major decisions.

Note also, that as an S Corp, you cannot offer multiple classes of stock (can only issue common stock), which can limit your attempts to raise capital. The costs of establishing an S Corp are also similar to those for a standard corporation.

# Chapter Two

## How Do You Save Money

Most entrepreneurs, the biggest incentive in setting up their company as an S corporation is to lower self employment taxes, as incorporating a business as an S Corp allows owners to avoid Social Security, Medicare or self-employment taxes on the part of the business profits. But how does setting up an S Corp enable tax avoidance? Let's find out below.

Let's say you have a small business that makes $100,000 a year in profits.

As you know, you pay income taxes to the federal government and, most likely, to your state government as well — the amount paid to the federal government as income tax depends on some factors.

If you are self-employed, your Social Security tax rate is 12.4 percent, and your Medicare tax is 2.9 percent. This brings the total tax rate for self-employment to 15.3%.

Now, assuming you have a friend who runs a sole proprietorship business that also happens to earn $100,000 in profits each year, the amount you will pay as tax will differ slightly from theirs, due to the S Corp advantage.

Your friend who owns a sole proprietorship will have to pay 15.3% of the self-employment taxes on the entire $100,000, which is $15,300.

For you, setting up your company as an S Corp makes you both the owner and employee. Now, assuming you assign yourself a "reasonable salary" of $6,670/month, this will give you a total wages of $80,040 per year, leaving the amount of your S corporation distribution as $19,960 per year. Since you only pay self-employment taxes on wages, you will pay the 15.3% tax on the total earned income of $80,040. $80,040 X 15.3% = $12,246.12.

Your friend who runs a sole proprietorship, on the other hand, will have to pay taxes on the entire $100,000. $100,000 X 15.3% = $15,300.

As an S-Corporation, therefore, you will pay $3,053.88 a year less than your friend in taxes. Being an S corporation saves you money by enabling you to split your business profits into two categories of "shareholder wages" and "shareholder distributions," of which the distributive share is not subject to self employment tax of 15.3%.

Often the savings can be much more significant than this depending on the amount of the business revenue and how much the shareholder needs paid in a "reasonable salary."

# Chapter Three

## Reasonable Salary

As an entrepreneur, being an owner of an S Corporation allows you to characterize your income for tax purposes. As seen above, being both the owner and shareholder of an S Corp means you can be an employee of the business and pay yourself a salary from the company, just like an employee would.

In addition to the salary you receive, you can also pay yourself dividends from the S Corp or distributions that are generally tax-free. This helps you lower your self-employment tax liability, as long as your salary and dividends/distributions are being characterized reasonably.

However, in an attempt to avoid paying self-employment taxes on the "dividend/distribution" portion of their income, some entrepreneurs pay themselves or their employees an artificially low salary, which is what the IRS tries to prevent. Instead, the IRS encourages S corporation shareholders who are owners or officers of the business to pay "reasonable salaries" to staff members who are actively involved in the day to day running of the business. But what exactly is a reasonable salary?

A reasonable usually refers to the 'market' salary someone would receive in a similar position at another company of same size and type. You can search and compare average salaries by job title on websites such as Theladders.com and Salary.com. Alternatively, you can hire a compensation consultant to assist with the analysis.

Also, you can research the level of wages in the industry in which your organization operates by confirming from sources like chambers of commerce, trade associations, industry reporting services or even your colleagues.

The IRS does not provide specific guidelines as to what constitutes a fair wage. However, you work your payment around some of the factors considered by courts when ruling on the matter. These factors include:

- The employee's training and experience
- The duties and responsibilities undertaken by the employee
- The worker's dedication regarding time and effort devoted to the business
- Compensation agreements
- The use of compensation formulas to determine compensation
- Dividend history

- Compensation paid to non-shareholder employees

- The frequency with which bonus is paid to key stakeholders

- What comparable companies pay their employees for similar services

# Chapter Four

## Shareholder Distributions

Shareholder distributions are one of the four ways an S-Corp shareholder takes money out of the business. The others are reasonable S Corp salary, self-rental, and reimbursements. When you transfer money from your business checking account to your personal checking account or write a check to yourself, you are taking a shareholder distribution.

When such payments are made to the shareholders, the distributions are tax-free. As a result, you are not taxed on the distributions nor are the distributions a deduction to the business. Instead, you are taxed on income of the business. And such income is taxed only once, irrespective whether it is distributed or left in the business.

Money accumulated in your business checking account is not regarded as profits and losses (P&L) since they passed through to shareholders and included on their individual tax returns.

Under Section 1368, cash or property distribution by an S Corp may lead to three possible tax consequences to the recipient shareholder:

- The distribution may result in a taxable dividend

- A tax-free reduction of the shareholder's basis in the company's stock

- Gain from the sale of the stock, resulting in capital gain

The aim of Section 1368 and the underlying regulations is to protect the main difference between C and S corporations, which stipulates that the earnings and profits (income) of C corporations must be taxed a second time when distributed, while that of an S corporation should not be taxed a second time.

It is crucial to understand the link between stock basis, previously-taxed income, earnings and profits, and the accumulated adjustments account to establish the taxability of an S Corp's distributions. Not doing so could further complicate the process and increase the chances of reaching the wrong conclusion.

Overall, it is the interaction between stock basis, profits and losses (P&L), and the accumulated adjustments account (AAA) that drive the taxability of an S corporation's distributions.

What are the S Corporation Distribution Rules Meant to Achieve?

Before you go on to set up an S Corp, it is essential first to understand precisely why distributions made by an S corporation are treated differently from those made by other ownership forms like C corporations.

A vital characteristic of subchapter C is the concept of "double taxation," where there are two levels of federal tax to pay. When a C corporation earns taxable income, such earnings are taxed at the corporate level. When the income is distributed, the distribution is again taxed to the shareholder as a dividend. Consequently, the same income which the company earned is taxed twice; one at the entity level and the second at the shareholder level.

As you may already know by now, S corporations differ from C Corporations in this regard because they are subject to a single level of taxation – the shareholder level. When an S Corp earns an income, that earning is typically not taxed at the entity level. Instead, the income generated is shared among the shareholders, who file and pay tax on their own share of the S Corp's earning on their individual income tax returns.

If the company decides to pay out dividends, the earnings are not taxed a second time under the single level of taxation specific to S corporations.

### How to Take Earnings Out of an S Corp

Business owners who run as S corporation can take money out of the corporation in a variety of ways:

## Wages

As mentioned, S corporation shareholders who work for the business, be they shareholder or employee, are classified as employees and receive the same tax treatment as any other staff who works for the company who is not a shareholder. This means that they are issued a paycheck, issued a W-2, pay employment taxes, etc.

Shareholders who work for a business incorporated into an S corporation should receive "reasonable" compensation for the services they render to the company.

## Distributions from S Corporation Earnings

When a regular C corporation pays out its earnings out of its retained earnings, such an allocation is known as a dividend. Shareholders of a C corporation are issued Form 1099-DIV by the organization to report such dividend. In turn, C corporation shareholders report the dividend on their individual income tax.

S corporations, on the other hand, do not make dividend distributions. Instead, they make non-dividend distributions, which are tax-free. However, for this to happen, the distribution must not exceed the shareholder's stock basis. In cases where the distribution exceeds the shareholder's stock basis, the excess amount is taxable as a long-term capital gain. Distributions made by an S Corporation are not subject to Social Security and Medicare taxes (FICA taxes).

# Chapter Five

## You have to be Organized

On the individual level, investing some extra time organizing your business enables you to make quick and reliable decisions both on the strategic and operative level.

The secret to having a well-run and appropriately-equipped company is organizing your business in such way that you are going to get all the necessary information that you need on time. That way you can make the right decisions and plan all your obligations without stress.

Here's how you can get it together:

## Keep Personal and Business Accounts Separate

One of the conventional wisdom of entrepreneurship is to never mix business and personal funds. A business should have its own account.

While there is no legal requirement to have a business bank account if you are a sole proprietor or partnership, it is important that you have a business account if you are incorporating into an S Corp.

Keeping your personal and business accounts separate can be quite useful especially for completing your tax returns and claiming expenses that can be offset against the profits made to lower your tax bill. On the other hand, combining the two will mean a mess at tax time.

Also, using a personal account for business will make you look unprofessional. Maintaining a separate business account also makes it easier for you to designate your business deductions and income clearly. For instance, if you want to be able to claim expenses as deductions, you must be able to show that the deductions made were for business purposes, and not personal expenses. Having a business account enables you to achieve this goal.

Besides, trying to sort through your personal records at tax time can be a nightmare. For easier operation, it will be wise to capture business expenses in your business account so you can easily claim deductions.

Here's how you can keep your business finances separate from personal ones:

## 1. Maintain separate checking accounts

Now that you know how important keeping a separate business account is, you can begin your journey to incorporation by opening a business checking account.

Having a separate business account gives the impression that you are a real business owner and not someone who's doing it as a hobby. It is the first thing that IRS looks to if there's ever a question about the status of your business.

If you use a finance management software program such as Quickbooks, Microsoft Money, or Quicken, it is also important to maintain separate systems for business and personal purposes.

Besides helping with tax issues, having two accounts will also improve your organization, as it helps you to keep everything in one place. Keeping records of your business finances by maintaining a separate account will give you proof of your business expenses if/when you get audited.

## 2.  Use a business credit card

Separating your personal and business finances should go beyond just keeping separate checking accounts. In addition to that, try to get a business credit card; it will also help with your organization and will come in when getting audited. Having a business credit card could also help with cash flow and provide you with an extra tax deduction.

## 3.  Incorporate your business

Now that your personal account is kept separate from your business account, the next step will be to establish an S Corp for your business.

Consult with your attorneys, accountants, insurance agents, and financial planners to identify the benefits of establishing as an S Corp and how this will impact your taxes. Setting up as an S Corp will give your finances a new level of liability protection since your business is treated as a separate entity.

## 4. File your taxes

With a checking account, credit card and record keeping software designed specifically for your business, you have everything that's needed to file your taxes.

Using a home office might qualify you to claim a home office deduction, meaning you can deduct expenses for the business use of your home. For this to apply, however, you must use the business part of your home exclusively and regularly for business purposes. Using the home office voluntarily, incidentally, or occasionally will not make you eligible for deductions.

The business part of your home must be used as your primary place of business, a place where you deal with clients in the normal course of your business, or a separate structure that you use in connection with your company.

## No Personal Expenses

We are constantly reminded that a business should be treated as a separate entity from our personal life. However, business owners tend to ignore this advice and go on to mix business and personal expenses all too often.

Some entrepreneurs make payments for their personal expenses out of the business checking account or use the business credit card for those personal expenses. Doing so can lead to IRS and legal issues. To avoid this, write checks for business purchases from the business account and personal purchases from the personal account.

Of course, the first step to achieving this goal is to put business income in the business account and personal income in the personal account, as mentioned above. Same should apply to credit card accounts – have one for business and one for personal use to avoid mixing charges or payments for these accounts.

Always bear in mind that the money that comes into the business is meant to be used strictly for business purposes. That means it should only be used for paying for business-related expenses such as business rents/utilities, supplies, payroll, as well as anything directly related to the running of the business.

Avoid using money from your business account to pay for personal expenses such as your mortgage, rent, personal vacations, debt payments for your debt repayment plan, or anything else that is not related to the business.

If you have a home office, you can take a reasonable portion of some household expenses such as auto-related expenses or utility bills (cable, cell, electricity, water, etc.).

That being said, sometimes, it is necessary to take money out of the business to cover some personal expenses. However, you have to ensure that you are doing this the right way. If you get caught mixing business and personal spending, you may be made to pay additional income taxes plus penalties and compromise the legal protection of your corporation.

As mentioned, you would have to undergo an audit if you get caught using business money for personal purposes. If the receipts or invoices that you provide fail to support your claims, the expenses will be added back to the tax return, after which your individual return will be recalculated.

Also, the additional income may make you ineligible for deductions and/or credits that were initially claimed. Also, your new income tax liability will be worked out, and you will again be made to pay penalties and interest on the unpaid part of this new figure.

As you can see, mixing business and personal expenses can be a dangerous game. Taking money out the correct way, on the other hand, would help you to avoid the onus of having to establish the expenses in question as valid business expenses.

So what's the correct way to get your money without creating a paper trail?

As an S Corp, if you need to access money for personal reasons, there are two acceptable methods for doing so: You either pay yourself through salary or write check to yourself in the form of distribution, as discussed earlier.

There should always be some form of separation between business and personal expenses, as doing otherwise will draw unnecessary attention to the transactions.

Also, it is crucial to set yourself up with regular payments, even if such payments aren't actual salary will make your business look more legitimate.

## Good Accounting Records

Keeping accurate records is a legal requirement for a business, and can help you to save money. Having good accounting records will help facilitate your tax planning and ensure you get the most out of your business.

Good record-keeping is critical to running a successful business. Having an accurate, organized records makes preparing your accounts at year-end easier, enables you to keep track of your company's cash flow, make good business decisions, as well as ensures you get to avoid headaches when you are filing your tax return.

Usually, your accounting records also consist of information about salaries and dividends and make it possible for you to keep on top of all business expenses.

When this is the case, you get to lower the amount of profit you will pay tax on. Besides, having a poorly kept data could result in a penalty from the IRS.

Here are some reasons to keep good financial records for your business:

## 1. Tracking the progress of your business

To run a business successfully, you need to be able to make decisions and design a roadmap that will enable you to accomplish your goals. For this to happen, you will need data, which can only be had keeping accurate, organized records.

It is only through information collected through record keeping that you can monitor how your business is performing over a certain period. Record keeping enables you to quickly establish how your business is doing at any particular moment.

After keeping good records regularly for a while, you will be able to see how your business is trending over time. You will then know what steps are needed to get you going in the right direction. Other than showing whether your business is improving, records also enable you to know which items are selling.

## 2. Prepare your financial statements

Record keeping makes it possible for you to have the information that you need to prepare your financial statements. Practicing business record keeping makes it easier for you to keep up with your profit and loss statement, so you know whether you are making or losing much, and how much you are making or losing.

Also, without the information from your accounting data, it will be impossible to prepare a balance sheet, which makes it difficult to identify your assets and liabilities. This information will make obtaining credit easier.

## 3. Identify Source of Receipts

As a business, you receive money or items from many sources. Without your records, it will be near impossible to identify the source of your receipts over time. Record keeping also makes it easier for you to determine your highest paying customers and reward their loyalty and strengthen your relationship with them. Having your records also makes it easier for you to identify your debtors and creditors.

Regarding tax, identifying your source of receipts enables you to separate business from your personal receipts, and taxable from nontaxable income.

## 4. Help prepare your tax returns

If the reasons mentioned above do not motivate you enough to keep records, this one sure would. Keeping records enables you to accurately be able to determine what your business earned in a financial year as well as the amount that you need to pay in taxes to the government. Not knowing your records could lead you to pay a lot more money in taxes than you normally would each year. Keeping good records also allows you to track all of your deductible business expenses. Doing so help ensures that you do not end up with a big tax bill. You need all the data you can collect to help your accountant make a case for you, since this data doesn't just come out of thin air.

## 5. Support items on your tax return

Generally, it is necessary to keep records that support an item of income or expenses. Keeping records of supporting documents such as sales slips, invoices, deposit slips, bills, receipts, and canceled checks provide support for the entries in your books and on your tax return.

Your supporting documents should show clearly the amount paid or earned and whether the payment or earned income was for purchases, sales, or services rendered. Having a complete set of records will help quicken the examination, giving you enough time to get back to your business.

**Steps to Take to Ensure Better Business Record Keeping**
Record keeping doesn't just happen; it takes careful planning and extensive practical preparation. Here are the steps you will have to take to ensure that all relevant records are kept:

## 1. Know exactly what you need to record

Typically, you should keep all records for a minimum of three years, although documents such as those containing information concerning a home sale/purchase, stock transactions, IRA and business or rental property should be kept longer.

As you would already know, you will have to file a tax return to tell the IRS how profitable your business has been as well as how much tax will be owed. You cannot do this accurately unless you keep records of all your business transactions such as:

## (i) Invoices

Invoices are used to monitor all of your income. Invoices should contain information about the transaction type, the date it was completed, the amount paid, as well as details regarding company addresses and registration number. Number each invoice in sequential order so that you can notice if there are any gaps in your records.

## (ii) Receipts

Monitoring your expenses is the best way to stay tax-compliant. Save any receipts concerning your business. These may include business lunches, travel expenses, office space, and supplies, among other things. Talk to your accountant for more information on what expenses you can claim.

You will also have to keep records of cashbooks, bank statements, as well as wage books. The exact documentation you will keep will depend on the type of business you run.

## 2. Download Managing and Record-Keeping Apps

As with all things, technology makes record keeping and organization a lot easier giving business owners a place to log and store information. The ability to enter data on a system makes management tasks and record keeping far more straightforward than having to go the manual route.

There are some useful apps, and many of these apps are free or cost under $20 a month, that will enable you to record your expenses and keep on top of invoicing. Some of these apps come with features that facilitate reporting and will remind you about late invoices.

This means that you need not keep a hard copy of your invoices and receipts since you can store everything online, which makes reporting income and expenses much easier and fun to do. This way, you get to track your business records and avoid any surprises that may arise when filing your tax return. Also, it is recommended to also record everything in real-time to prevent them from slipping through. Also, ensure to back up your data as often as possible so that you can protect and restore your data when something goes wrong. The good thing is many of these software programs are backed up in the cloud.

## 3. Keep business and personal finances separate

The fact that you have to treat your business as a separate entity, regardless of its size, cannot be emphasized enough. It's recommended to open a separate bank account for your business funds and to use this for expenses that are related to the business.

Doing so help ensures that you don't confuse money spent on your business and personal life or spend time separating the two in the future. Besides, maintaining a separate account for your business will also help you to understand better what concerns the company and could prevent you from being accused of tax avoidance by the IRS.

As an S Corp, you must ensure you are tax compliant, which means maintaining records of every transaction you make. Doing so helps to give you better financial control over your business's growth and success and will help make sure that you have nothing to worry about when dealing with the IRS.

## Pay Yourself Wages

Establishing as an S corporation allows you to enjoy a special tax status granted by the IRS, which is made possible due to the business' small number of shareholders (not more than 100). S-Corporations are not subject to corporate tax rates and are exempt from federal income taxes. Instead, they pass income and losses through to these shareholders who are then taxed on their individual returns.

The special tax treatment enjoyed by S Corps allows shareholders to potentially take money out of the either in the form of a tax-free distribution of profits or as taxable salary.

The tax agency requires business owners and shareholders who work for an S Corp to pay themselves a "reasonable" salary, rather than take all earnings and profits out of the company as distributions.

The advantages of paying yourself wages as an S Corp include:

## Audit Avoidance

The main benefit of paying salary as an S corporation business is to avoid coming under the scrutiny of the IRS and a potential audit. As mentioned, wages paid to employees of an S Corporation are subject to self employment taxes. In the past, S corporation shareholders avoided paying self employment taxes by sharing earnings in the form of tax-free distributions, even though some shareholders were active employees of the organization.

As you would expect, this practice resulted in a decrease in employment tax withholdings. To curtail this, the Internal Revenue Service declared that shareholder-employees must pay themselves a fair salary before profits are distributed. A company that fails to pay what is considered a reasonable salary could result in interest and penalties and re-characterization of previous distributions to wages.

## Business Deductions

As an S corporation, salaries payment, as well as the employment taxes, are regarded as a deductible business expense. Tax-free distributions to shareholders are not viewed as a business expense, and consequently, are not tax-deductible.

Hence, paying a salary that is considered a business expense more properly reveals the cost of doing business and makes it possible for your financial statements to demonstrate your company's current financial position better.

Not paying salaries artificially reduces your organization's operational needs.

## Business Credit

As an S corporation, you are more likely to qualify for business credit when you pay salaries than when you don't pay. The payment of payroll is seen as a sign that your company is in good financial health, regardless of whether salaries are being only to owner-employees.

Other than the fact that it demonstrates your company's financial stability, your company's bank and payroll processor can also serve as business references, since they consider payroll to be a continual transaction process that transfers large sums through their financial institutions.

## Withholdings

Salaries payment offers benefits to shareholder-employees in that employment taxes are considered a type of forced savings and contribution toward retirement. Paying taxes as an employee enables you to contribute your share toward Social Security and Medicare for your future needs, and as a result, you will often receive a lump sum state and federal tax refund.

Also, the payment of salary and employment taxes serves as income verification when an employee is applying for a loan or mortgage.

### Quarterly Payroll Tax Returns – Fed 941, State, Unemployment

Form 941 is a crucial payroll tax form that enables business owners to report on what they have been withholding regarding federal income taxes and Social

Security/Medicare taxes, employer payments for these withholding amounts, as well as any amounts due to the IRS.

**Form 941 Due Dates**

As mentioned, Form 941 is due four times a year, at the end of the month following the end of the quarter. The schedule is as follows:

- For the first quarter of a specific year, say 2019, ending March 31, submit by April 30

- For the second quarter, ending June 30, you're expected to provide by July 31

- For the third quarter, ending September 30, you will need to submit by October 31

- For the fourth quarter, ending December 31, you have to file by January 31, 2020.

When the due date falls on a weekend or holiday, submissions will be accepted without penalty on the next business day. For example, if the April 30 due date is a Sunday for that year, the due date for that payment would be Monday, May 1.

Employers who have completed their payroll tax deposits for the quarter on time have ten more days after the stated due dates to file form 941 for the quarter.

Form 941 can be filed electronically using Federal E-file.

It is necessary to make either monthly or semi-weekly deposits, depending on the amount owed. So you do not have to wait until you file Form 941 to pay all taxes for the quarter at that time.

Employers who have paid the whole amount of their payroll taxes during the months covered by the Form 941 will see "$0" due when they attempt to pay taxes with

Form 941. However, those who were required to make deposits may have a balance due.

### Annual Wage Reporting – W2/W3 Fed 940

Each employer must provide each employee an annual report on IRS Form W-2 (Wage and Tax Statement). The form captures wages paid as well as Federal, state and local taxes withheld.

The form is used to report the payments made to employees in the form of wages as well as the taxes withheld from them. Form W-2 reports FICA taxes (Social Security and Medicare) to the Social Security Administration (SSA). In turn, the SSA reports appropriate amounts on the form to the IRS.

An employer legally must send out W-2 Forms to each of its employees to whom they paid a salary, wage or another form of compensation. Note that this does not include contracted or self-employed workers, who are expected to file taxes with different forms (1099s).

The W-2 form reports income from January 1 through December 31 of each year, irrespective of the fiscal year used by the employer or employee for other tax purposes. Note that such filing is made about the period in which an employee has been compensated, and not necessarily the actual dates of their employment. An employer is required to keep copies of W-2 forms for up to four years.

Employers are required to send Copies B, C, 1, and 2 to their staff by January 31 of the year immediately following the year of income to which Form W2 relates. Employers are expected to electronically file Form W-2 Copy A with the SSA by January 31.

Forms W-2 and W-3 forms can also be submitted by paper mail. Employers are required to submit both tax forms at the same time.

It is recommended that you verify that your data are accurate before you send off these tax forms to the SSA. Also, ensure that the totals on Tax Form W-3 equal the amounts on your W-2s. You might also want to double-check to ensure that your name, address, and employer ID number are correct.

**Annual 1120S Filing**

Form 1120S is a tax document used by S Corps to report the income, losses, and dividends of their shareholders. The form, which is part of the Schedule K-1 document, establishes the percentage of company shares that belong to each shareholder for the tax year. The authorities require that this form is prepared for all individuals.

You can either download the form and complete it manually or use tax software such as TurboTax or with your tax professional. The due date for the form is March 15.

As mentioned, income from S corporation returns passes through to the shareholders. As a result, late filing of the 1120S makes it difficult for shareholders to meet their own filing obligations on time. To prevent such issue, the authorities have imposed some substantial penalties for late filing of the 1120S.

The penalty **per shareholder** is $195 per month. However, individuals with a clean history and no penalties can get the penalty abated through a first-time penalty abatement.

The business can get a six month extension on filing the 1120S by filing Form 4868. This would extend the due date until 9/15. While you get the extension none of the shareholder's will have the necessary information to complete their personal tax returns.

# Chapter Six

## Deductions and Tactics Once You're an S-Corp

While it is necessary to pay taxes, you do not have to pay more than you must. Tax deductions can help to reduce your bill by thousands of dollars, provided you can adequately account for the relevant expenses

Thankfully, there are some potential tax moves that can save your business money. We discuss them below.

## Augusta Loophole

You may or may not know this, but there's a loophole in the tax code which, beyond just exempting your income from taxation, enable you not even to report your earnings to the IRS at all. This move is commonly known as the Augusta Loophole, a strategy that allows you to rent out your residence for up to 14 nights per year without reporting the income.

Affluent homeowners in Augusta, Georgia are often credited for the tax exemption on fourteen nights or less of rental income in a primary residence. Each year, Augusta residents rented their homes at a premium to tourists and golfers who go to the city to watch the best golfers compete in a golf tournament known as The Masters.

When the federal government tried to collect a share of the money the residents received from rent, they (the residents) appealed to Congress to exclude these funds from their taxable income. This gave rise to what is now commonly referred to as the Master's rule, which stipulates that individuals who rent their home for fourteen nights a year or less do not need to report the income they earn from doing so.

As an S Corp, The Master's rule gives you an opportunity to capture easy, tax-free income. One way to earn such tax-free income is to have the business hold a monthly meeting in your personal residence and pay rent for it. By so doing, you monetize your space with no tax implications. To make sure you can prove your income is tax-free you have to keep detailed records and minutes of the meetings.

## Have the Business Reimburse You for Mileage or Own the Vehicle

If you use your personal vehicle for business purposes, you can recover some of the money you spend on gas and vehicle maintenance. This can be achieved in the following ways:

- Actual expense method: Under this method, the deductible costs are calculated based on the amount spent on gas, tires, repairs, oil, and insurance. Using this method, you can also deduct depreciation expenses on the vehicle being used.

- Standard mileage rate: Under this approach, you can deduct a fixed amount for each mile driven. Parking fees and tolls, which are also tax deductible, fall under this category.

## Have the Business Rent Home Office

Getting your business to rent home office enables you to deduct the cost of maintaining the home office. In the past, entrepreneurs had to compute all their expenses, establish the actual percentage of the home used for business purposes, and then multiply the two to determine the tax deduction.

Nowadays, all you have to do is multiply the square footage of your home office (up to a maximum of 300 sq. ft.) by $5.

To take advantage of this tax deduction method, you have to ensure that the home office area must is used exclusively for business purposes, as mentioned in the previous chapter.

As a S Corp your business can enter into a lease agreement with you personally and pay a flat rate of rent monthly to you.

# Chapter Seven

## Steps to Take

To form an official business, you must take these essential steps:

**File for LLC, Corporation, or Professional Corporation with Your State Depending On Your Business**

The first step to take is to visit your state's Secretary of State website and look for the "corporations" section on the site, then navigate to the corporations forms. While you are there, look for the form concerning filing the articles of incorporation.

Complete the articles of incorporation form and write out the name of the business. Such name must include any of the following words: "corporation," "limited," "incorporated," or "company." After that, you will have to state the number of shares of stock that the business allowed to issue.

Provide the registered address of the business as well as the name of its registered agent. If the company has a principal office that isn't the registered office, provide the address of the principal office.

Also, it is required that the corporation has at least one incorporator. Hence, you will have to provide the incorporator's name and address. If many, you need to give all of their names and addresses and have each incorporator sign the articles of incorporation.

File the form and pay the required filing fee. How you will submit the form differ depending on your state of residence. Some states accept applications online, while others require you to mail the form and accompanying payment to the office of the Secretary of State.

If you are mailing the articles of incorporation, use the address published on the website. Complete a "Return Receipt after Mailing" form at your post office. Doing so guarantees that the Secretary of State receives the articles. Also, you can personally convey the articles of incorporation to the Secretary of State to ensure receipt.

## Get EIN with IRS

The next step is to apply for an Employer Identification Number (EIN) with the Internal Revenue Service. You need a valid Taxpayer Identification Number (SSN, ITIN, EIN) to able to apply for EIN. You can apply online, by mail, telephone, or fax. Further information regarding the application can be found here https://www.irs.gov/businesses/small-businesses-self-employed/how-to-apply-for-an-ein.

## Get Tax IDs with Your State

A state tax ID enables business owners to pay their state business taxes and withhold state income taxes from staff paychecks if their state has an income tax. Though issued by states, the tax ID is similar to a federal employer identification number, and serves as a unique identifier for your organization in tax filings.

While the process of getting tax IDs vary slightly across states, the IDs are issued by a state official, usually the secretary of state. To get your ID, therefore, you will need to visit the website of the secretary of state, then find the corporation or business division.

Download the state tax ID form and fill it out with the required details, then return same to the secretary of state by following the directions on the form.

You will be notified by the state when your ID has been issued.

## File IRS Form 2553

When you form a corporation, the IRS automatically assumes that it's a C corporation unless you go the extra mile. This is because, upon formation, all corporations are treated as C corps by default. As a result, you have to take the extra step of electing S corporation status. Failure to do this will see you pay a corporate income tax on your net taxable income for the year.

This is where the IRS Form 2553 comes in handy, as it is used for gaining recognition under Subchapter S of the federal tax code. The form can be downloaded for free from www.irs.gov/pub/irs-pdf/f2553.pdf and should be submitted by mail or fax.

The form must be filed before the 16th day of the third month of the corporation's tax year (within 75 days of formation) for the election to take effect from the date of establishment. Alternatively, you can file before the 15th day of the second month of a tax year if the tax year is two-and-a-half months or less. Generally, calendar year corporations have until 2/15 to make the election and it be retroactive to the beginning of the year. Late filings of this form are often accepted by the IRS if a reasonable cause is given.

Business owners can also file the form at any time during the tax year before the year in which they want the election to take effect.

## Conclusion

An S Corp is a great business structure for small business owners that want to protect themselves from liability, enjoying the benefits of pass-through income, and savings on self-employment tax. If you do not mind the strict requirements that are imposed on S corporations, then establishing as an S Corp is a great option to consider. The savings can often be quite substantial and be more than enough to pay for a professional to complete all the filings that are needed to stay in good standing.

**About the Author**

Paden Squires is a licensed CPA in the state of Missouri. He specializes in working with real estate agents and investors across the country in helping them not only conduct their business in the most tax beneficial way, but also succeed in all aspects of business. For questions or comments email info@squirescpa.com.